Ceaseless Rain

Ceaseless Rain
DOROTHY MAHONEY

Copyright © 2020 Dorothy Mahoney
All rights reserved

Palimpsest Press
1171 Eastlawn Ave. Windsor, Ontario. N8S 3J1
www.palimpsestpress.ca

Book and cover design by Dawn Kresan. Typeset in Adobe Garamond Pro, and printed offset on Zephyr Laid at Coach House Printing in Ontario, Canada. Edited by Dawn Kresan.

Palimpsest Press would like to thank the Canada Council for the Arts, and the Ontario Arts Council for their support of our publishing program. We also acknowledge the assistance of the Government of Ontario through the Ontario Book Publishing Tax Credit.

LIBRARY AND ARCHIVES CANADA CATALOGUING IN PUBLICATION

Title: Ceaseless rain / Dorothy Mahoney.
Names: Mahoney, Dorothy, 1957–, author.
Description: Poems.

Identifiers: Canadiana (print) 20200173790
　　　　　　Canadiana (ebook) 20200173839

ISBN 9781989287392 (softcover)
ISBN 9781989287408 (EPUB)
ISBN 9781989287415 (Kindle)
ISBN 9781989287422 (PDF)

Classification: LCC PS8576.A446 C43 2020 | DDC C811/.54—DC23

for those who help

Vocabulary of rain

13	Vocabulary of rain
14	Blue Monday
15	Hospice duty
16	The man in Room 5 is no longer eating
17	M PATHY
18	In the pink
19	Neapolitan
20	A raisin kind of day
21	Talking to the dead man
22	In February
23	When I open the jar of Manitoulin honey
24	Kispiox honey
25	Waiting
26	Heat
27	No need for shoes
28	*You follow?*
29	Resolve
30	The last word

Encyclopedia of rain

33	Encyclopedia of rain
35	The map of sorrow
36	"Death happens. It's what you do after that counts."
37	Grief
38	Someone else cooks breakfast
39	My son tells me about his friend's sister's boyfriend's brother
40	When the pandemic started
41	One for sorrow
42	Common red polls
43	Ortolan bunting
44	Lapis lazuli

45	Lazuli bunting
46	The last words of parrots
47	Reaching for Monet's water lilies
48	Inheritance
49	A gift of tea from China
50	The visitors
51	My father's Christmas card
52	Dinner
53	My mother waters the yard
54	Cleaning out the kitchen
55	Mrs. Klein's dishes
56	Copying Mrs. B's cake recipe displayed at her visitation
57	The dog that won't cross over
58	My sister in the cemetery
59	Small hands
60	The year I was born they buried a Plymouth Belvedere
63	Acknowledgements
65	Author Biography

nobody, not even the rain, has such small hands

—e. e. cummings
  "somewhere i have never travelled, gladly beyond"

Vocabulary of rain

Vocabulary of rain

We forget.
It pools in hollows
of curled leaves
against the closed gate.

Even yesterday's teacup
becomes a rain gauge.

Drop
it speaks in monologues.
Drip
it slurs steady,
sliding down the chain
to fill the barrel.

It's what we wish for
when there is none,
curse
when it continues.

It soaks through our shoes
staining our steps
with now.

Blue Monday

It is already Tuesday when I read in the paper
that Monday was the worst day of the year.
On Wednesday I hear the story of how
your cousin died.

Sadness is a plummeting emptiness,
the way the floor drops in carnival rides
and you're sucked to the wall and can't move,
face pulled by the cheeks and you can't speak.
Grief a spinning force.

Closing your eyes makes it worse.
There are no greeting cards for this.
The barker shouts, "Balloons! Peanuts!"
Only when you see the elephant
do you cry.

Hospice duty

Arrive early. Sign in. Secure
belongings in the locker.
This is the time of thaw: soup from the freezer,
chili, names of the recent deceased.
Soon nurse and cart will stop
at each doorway, assess pain.
Coffee brews,
cookies lined in rows of three
by kind, smocks cover otherworld clothing.
Can I help you?
What do you need? What can I do?
Laugh but not too loud.
Sanitize your hands and wear gloves. Don't
take gifts from the dying.

The man in Room 5 is no longer eating

What's left is between us. We lower the side rails of the bed, the clanging like a gate closing, closed. Without words, we remove the pillows that keep him in place, nestled artifact: crockery, pale, crackled; folded feather; slivered sigh on rock. No rain now for some weeks. Trees shed their leaves and it feels like October in July. Soon visitors will arrive. We turn him, gentle, with gloved hands.

swabbing his mouth
under the tongue, and over

M PATHY

This is the license plate on the car ahead of me as I drive home from my shift. A woman stayed in Room 1 while we washed her mother, a broken bird with bone cancer, arms bent against bare chest, fingers darkened, no longer able to hold on to things. The daughter talks about her heart and her head, how her mother wanted to die at home, and her heart tugs but her head knows she cannot care for her. Each movement starts a whimper, hip fractured, head curled against neck. *This is what it comes to,* she says. *You do what you can do.* You do.

cracked cup
slow leak
across the counter

In the pink

She is bounce-hop-skipping-jumping in her pink shoes. Her blonde hair swings and twirls. She is four and visiting her Pup-pa. She has been to a birthday party and thrusts each treasure from her pink bag across the bed so he can see, but not close enough to touch. Gumballs in a miniature machine, a rainbow-swirl lollipop, a roll of sweet tarts, a granola bar, a sandwich bag of cherry tomatoes. Pup-pa laughs. She tells him about the doll with a dress that was the cake, the dress was the cake! He asks if she brought him a piece. She is ready to colour the whole world pink.

carnations
on the nightstand
a get-well card

Neapolitan

He asks for ice cream every morning after breakfast. Three, make it six, scoops will do. There is a larger bowl reserved for him with a larger spoon so he can slide it easily into his mouth, like the oatmeal, like the scrambled eggs. One morning he decides he can no longer stay in bed. His thin legs flail from the sheet. He must get up. But he can't. *What do I have to look forward to? What? Tell me that.* We say, ice cream. *Maple Walnut.*

vanilla moon
strawberry dawn
dark rooftops

A raisin kind of day

It can't be that hard. The kitchen volunteer googles rice pudding on her phone. The woman in Room 2 would like some for breakfast. There is no rice pudding in the cupboard, not behind the stacked pudding cups, not mixed with the cans of fruit cocktail. Now she searches for rice. *It must be like making risotto, the "food of love," because you can't leave it to do something else. You must lock eyes on it.* Stirring, stirring. It begins to thicken. She adds raisins. Too late for the man in Room 6 who would eat some but only if it's plain.

warm blanket
the difference between
marmalade and jam

Talking to the dead man

The brother tells his father that the room is best kept cold. The son is on the bed, eyes closed. His family moves to stand outside so we can wash him, but first his mother hands us his favourite sport shirt. I tell him this is lucky, ask who won the final match. His arm bends easily into the sleeve. My co-worker is slipping the shirt over his head and tells me they've called the funeral home, but I continue to talk about the morning haze, how birds come to the feeder, how the last of the senses is hearing. How very much he is loved.

at his side
no one wanting
to turn off the remote

In February
(Manuscript painting by the Limburg brothers, 1415)

Here in the *Very Rich Book of Hours*,
snow rests on the woven beehives, the plaited fence, the thatched roof
with the hole above the crowded sheep, weaving amongst themselves.
There is snow on the distant hills and on the church spire.
Today bees are scarce, churches sold, chainsaws have clear cut the woods
where this man hews and bundles kindling with bare hands.
It is not easy to stay warm in February.
Inside they perch before a fire, their garments raised,
their hands stretched out, blessed by warmth.
This is the same month, two brothers froze when their furnace stopped,
a boy died in a snowbank, and a roof collapsed in Alberta
killing five cows.
The man is painted behind a donkey loaded with sticks posed towards town.
Perhaps he will sell it for bread or wine; perhaps he will stay the night,
perhaps he will return.

When I open the jar of Manitoulin honey

It is February, the small jar with a label of bees
at the back of the cupboard
purchased during
a blur of July afternoons bordered by
the zigzag of split-rail fences
driving stretches of grazing cows
with no sight of anything miniscule as bees
or even bigger, bee boxes.
No remembrance of clover or sunflower
yet the luxury
of summer tenured in gold.

Slow drip from spoon over
slabs of fresh bread.
Abandoned apiary behind the barn
my grandfather's bee-keeping days
like the long-ago recipe of my grandmother's
honey cake.
The bees hollow in their winter darkness
having succumbed to moths or mice.
One jar, a triumph of last summer.

Kispiox honey

It was light in colour
like the lemon juice in a jar
next to the plate of red salmon
that came from the Kispiox river
that very morning
when he went fishing
and I went to the farmers' market
where the old man warned of wax particles,
his eight-sided jars clouded, unpasteurized,
as other hives were dying
he said his bees were happiest
as he fed them back their honey
instead of sugar in winter
and the Kispiox honey
was as sweet
as the salmon was red.

Waiting

This morning the coordinator corrals the volunteers.
She tells us a woman has applied for medical assistance in dying.
She says if that makes us uncomfortable,
to let her know. Some
volunteers are uneasy
about that, she explains, they don't want
to serve that last meal
or dress someone for the last
time. She says it won't happen here,
that the patient will be moved
somewhere off site.
She smiles reassuringly,
The approval takes some time,
perhaps she will change her mind.

Heat

The woman in Room 4 is sleeping with a washcloth on her forehead. The length of her is covered in a thin blanket except for her feet which are bare. Her toes stiff, pointed as if she were a ballerina. The nurse asks her husband if she had a fever during the night. He nods. Questions if he should change the temperature of the room. The weather outside has turned. It is no longer hot. He had to find a jacket this morning. The nurse says whatever makes him most comfortable, that an elevated temperature is normal as her body prepares to shutdown. He seems bewildered. Asks if Tylenol would help.

falling leaves
her socks
in his pocket

No need for shoes

It's self-sustaining, he says of the amaryllis blooming bare bulb against the window, a triumphant red. His daughter brought it. He has a catheter, no longer rises from bed, still likes to spread jam on his toast, sips coffee. *Close the door if you please,* he says, *I'm going to try to sleep. That's one thing I still do well.*

waning moon
light in the hallway
never goes out

You follow?

Listen. You understand? He speaks five languages. He says next spring he will be in the garden. In his country, his father and his grandfather grew grapes. Every four years they are grafted. He does not say this word but mimes it with his hands; one hand is the knife, the other the vine. *Perhaps he means 'cut back'?* He continues. *You need sheep manure. The grapes from here are sweet but the best grapes are sweet and have acid.*

hard frost
in many languages
good-bye sounds the same

Resolve

Sugar feeds cancer, they say, so I'm cutting back on candy. She is pulling a wig over the top of her head. Tugs at the strands. Soon she will slowly walk to the kitchen for more tea. *I'm leaving at the end of the month. The new place has a patio and my brother got me a bistro set. It's a nice place. Everyone is happy there. They play Bingo every day.* We cheer her on. She will rise, returning to the world.

autumn breeze
the kite trembles
in bare branches

The last word

New Year's Eve and Mike the bartender agrees
to make his signature drink.
Gin or tequila?
He flips two martini glasses,
fills them with ice.
He climbs the stepstool
to reach the top shelf,
takes down a bottle.
Dumps the ice.
Opens the jar of dark cherries,
and, smiling, starts to
measure-mix liquids.
Sip it, it's strong,
he advises.
It's called the Last Word.
It comes from Detroit
where it's called the Final,
but I've tweaked it.
He is self-taught.
The drink glows
green phosphorescence.
Smooth, it is smooth
like a good-bye
when you know you aren't
really leaving

just yet.

Encyclopedia of rain

Encyclopedia of rain

When no one would take them,
the Funk and Wagnall New Encyclopedia set
with the gilded edges, 1-25
were left at the curb for recycling;
side-by-side as if still on the shelf
alphabetical except for
25 Watfo-Zymol and the two volume Index
placed on top in a sturdy wide box
that once held bananas shipped
to the grocery store that sold cloth bags
to encourage green thinking.
It rained, all night.
The books, unwanted
like a litter
of kittens thrown into
the river.
Bound tightly, cover-
to-cover,
only the gilded edges,
the center columns, unrippled.
Dry. The inner sanctum of knowledge,
reverence like a whisper in a cathedral
of pages. *No food. No gum. Clean hands.*
One book after another to attain
all that was fact, all that was known
and mattered, alphabetical.
When selling them was a job going door-to-door;
like vacuum cleaners,

the customer shamed by the dirt the new model
found in seeming immaculate carpets.
When no one wanted to look impoverished,
ignorant, in neighbourhoods of carports and green lawns.
When there were titles like Fuller-Brush Man
who gave free shoe-horn samples,
3-D business cards, his name and number
pressed against the heel. When shoe store salesmen
measured your feet for fit;
ripped laces replaced, heels tipped with new lifts,
soles resoled. Leather polished and buffed,
when quality mattered above style and all questions
found reliable answers in the encyclopedia.
The rain continues. I hope the sodden box
will hold the weight. Better they sail
together into the giant bin of all that is waste:
butcher paper, brand-new shoe boxes,
birthday cards, egg cartons, envelopes,
scented stationary, heart-shaped chocolate boxes,
banana boxes, all recycled into what the world needs.

The map of sorrow

is well-creased, fold
after
                fold.

        An origami heart refusing
to resume the same shape
      each time it is smoothed over.

Others want to give directions, well-meaning
                detours,
a casserole covered in foil.

                You are here.

The roads washed out, culverts flooding,
      and the windshield wipers pulse faster than the heart.
There's no seeing past it.

"Death happens. It's what you do after that counts."

I hear this on the radio while driving and think
as survivor or deceased?

What are the dead allowed?
One final phone call,
one pressing question answered.
Revelation of what was in arrears,
to float through thoughts
to levy how little really mattered:
sum up what was donated, discarded.
The cash divided.
Where is the clock radio,
the ball peen hammer,
the silver-plated platter
that was a wedding gift.
Where will it go?

What do the dead do, after?
Meet at a common table,
acknowledge what was best,
reconnect coincidence,
recompense.
Imagine laughter.

Then I hear the word repeated,
debt,
not death, debt happens.
I have arrived, park the car
in an empty space.

Grief

The last apples
in the orchard
encased
by the ice
storm.

All that was
inner apple
becomes soft
slipping
from the skins.

This is grief;
whole yet hollow.
Ghost apples.

Someone else cooks breakfast

> *Let's not get romantic or dismal about death.*
> *Indeed, it is our most unique act along with birth.*
> *We must think of it as cooking breakfast*
> —JIM HARRISON, *Death Again*

We go out for breakfast
after the doctor's appointment.
The waitress asks, where do we want
to sit, and everything ordinary,
is no longer that. She pours
coffee into that moment.
Dark. Rich.
Asks, are we ready?
Over-easy is how I like it.
Over-easy, please.

My son tells me about his friend's sister's boyfriend's brother

It is the same morning I find the dead warbler
limp beneath the window, its thin legs drawn back
as if with no last thought of ever standing.
Tight beak, eyes dry pinpricks of last trees and lawns,
a body yellow green like new leaves of
the locust stretching towards our roof,
a tree that took so long to grow, we were never sure.
Such slow budding, while all else was deep green.
This brother, so young to leave in spring, or any season,
to have come so far, to hang from a barn rafter,
a yellow flash in a world too green.

When the pandemic started

They told us: self-isolate,
cough into your elbows,
scrub your hands.

In other countries, patients on ventilators
die alone; corpses stacked in refrigerated trucks.
There are no funerals.

Our can opener breaks. Before us, cans we could not open,
expiry dates sealed.

One for sorrow

This is how it begins,
counting crows,
throwing down sticks,
shuffling cards,
swirling tea leaves,
lines crisscross palms.
We want a sign.
Thin bones
in the sediment
of the birdbath,
keep us seeking
one more crow.

Common red polls

Suddenly they descend
seven of them,
in a flurry, new snow twirling.
They settle on the railing
the top of their heads, red
as if they struck the window
and miraculously survived.
Their breasts flecked crimson;
the framed colour plate
of Christ
in the church basement
his bare heart
arrow-pierced

red polls lifting.

Ortolan bunting

They say you can still eat them,
if you know the right people,
the right places. The tiny ortolan netted
illegally in France, blinded, force-fed:
grain, figs. Weeks later drowned
in brandy, eaten whole
beneath a napkin
placed over the diner's head
to enhance the aroma,
hide bone extraction.
To ask forgiveness.
Such is ritual,
tasting blood
when bones puncture
the mouth
but swallowing anyway.

Lapis lazuli

These are the teeth
that remain of the mouth
that held the lips
of a medieval nun
that shaped the brush
that held the dye
that coloured the blue
of the Virgin's robe
on vellum.

These are the flecks
of ultramarine
dug from the mines
in Afghanistan
traded in Venice
shipped to a monastery
where this nun
pleased with the page
vowed praise
as the blue
on her teeth
calcified.

Lazuli bunting

Now I study sparrows closely
as they flit through hedge-gaps
descend on fallen seeds
and ascend as quickly
with junco and chickadee.

Just four days ago
in zero temperature
a woman saw a bird
with white wing bars
and a spot of blue:

a lazuli bunting,
which should be wintering
in Mexico.
How often you see
only sparrows
because that's all you
think you see.

Come spring
how brilliant blue
the bunting.

The last words of parrots

Somewhere in the jungle
of the Orinoco River
parrots knew the lost language
of a vanished tribe, kept
captive by their conquerors
who didn't understand
what words they mimicked,
what meaning, what portend.

When Alex, the famous parrot
of 150 words died in 2007,
his last words:
you be good,
see you tomorrow, I love you.

Reaching for Monet's water lilies

I have seen these flowers
in northern ponds where pike
rise to pull ducklings down
and when I wanted to wade out
to pick pale petals, my aunt
would twist an undertow of
monsters lurking in the muck
and tangle.

There is no horizon
no bank below,
here in pastel peace
water lilies float in blue heavens,
unencumbered infinity.

I feel small again
knowing he painted these
after the death of a wife,
a son, his eyesight dimming,
when despair
was a ravenous pike.

Inheritance

It wasn't about the walnut table, not really.
A table's just a surface, somewhere flat
to grease a rifle, shine boots, fill mason jars with beets.
And since they all had tables,
it should have stayed in the sold house.

Perhaps, that is the start. One family table,
fists and spilled salt, mould around the mouth of sealed jars,
who claims the river, who the neighbour's barn, whose
words define you.

It wasn't about that, no, not really.

It was the axe splintering wood,
the bonfire behind the house,
dull boots kicking against the grain.

A gift of tea from China

How like a poem,
Ganpu:
a hollowed orange
hand-filled
with loose tea,
dried in the sun.

In the quiet serenity
of bird paradise,
mandarin trees
in rich soil
of the Pearl Delta,
so far from here.

Lift it from the paper,
hold it in your palm,
wake it with the first rinse.
Close your eyes,
breathe in,
let remembrance steep.

The visitors

My friend explains the end of life
in her faith. Expect two visitors, she says.
The first is the Angel of Forgetfulness,
to take away memory, like clearing dishes
from the table, one by one, the platters scraped
clean, the cutlery collected, shaking out the words
for everything tasted, no hunger left, even the body neglected.
The second is Silence, to dim the light,
pull the blinds, lead you through the door.

My father's Christmas card

how many times it crossed the ocean
a joke between men, the same Christmas card
with warm regard, a few more lines added,
a chuckle when read, and then to commit
to returning it, the next December;
nothing else surer, than its continuance
and now the significance, that it spans no more:
abandoned metaphor

Dinner

I would like to sit across from my father
while he sucked garlic snails from shells.
I would study his lowered head,
the way his hair whitened, grown sparse
and yet he grew it long to conceal the bald spot,
his fingers
thick and calloused, having hefted
mortar, block; a master in the art of building walls.

I hunger

for the way he held his knife and fork,
the way he palmed his cognac glass,
chewed the end of his cigar
patting pockets for matches.
How spare his instructions:
a lady never finishes her drink
walk don't run
don't ever let me hear you crying

and now this glass, how empty,
the table brushed of crumbs,
the other chair pushed in,
lights dim.

He is gone, but I have not eaten.

My mother waters the yard

While I'm away
my mother will step over
the flower beds
to see what I have
and haven't done.
The thistles she gave me, gone.
I used shovel, gloves,
their silver slivers
once under the skin
festering.
So much that needed water:
wave petunias,
hydrangeas,
morning glories,
four o'clocks with seeds
like small grenades.
She will dead head my roses, pull
tulip leaves from bulbs. She will stop
squirrels from digging, with rocks. Stride
my short comings. Find my secateurs,
save them from rusting in rain.

Cleaning out the kitchen

My mother-in-law's rolling pin
is heavy in the hand. A solid weight
of maple with two handles to even
the dough, for her apple pies, tourtieres,
and things she made before I knew her.
She liked to say it was easy, whatever she
had mastered.

Newly married, we would
call to see when pies came out of the oven,
then drive across town. Her kitchen clean;
the pull-out bread board back under the counter,
the dusting of flour gone from surfaces, hands.
Shaken apron, swept floor and the rolling pin
put away. Warm cinnamon, apple.

The smell of cleansers biting, no one finds an apron,
and if her apple pie recipe came from book or memory,
the youngest will never taste it, can
never beg a second piece, the measure of her joy.

Mrs. Klein's dishes

Pick-up trucks line the highway on either side coming out of Evansville, and an auction sign blocks the driveway. Men lean against the tractor, the boat, and the ice-fishing hut. They stand in groups around the tools, the tackle boxes, the paddles. There are six sets of moose antlers mounted and a fox pelt. There are minnow traps and axes. Wives are few but some judge folded linens, towels, bedsheets. She had three sets of dishes: Rose Bouquet, gold-rimmed Wedgwood blue, and another hidden in a box behind canisters full up with icing sugar, flour, rice. A few saucers missing. No longer balancing cups, they hold change, ashes.

Copying Mrs. B's cake recipe displayed at her visitation

Handwritten in German,
some words the same:
vanilla, butter, pudding, rum.

Breaking a dozen eggs,
one broken half holds the other.

First egg whites foam, froth, whip
into soft peaks, until you can turn
the bowl over and nothing falls out.

Somethings have no measure:
one package baking powder,
one package vanilla sugar.

Sometimes you must improvise:
mill the nuts in the coffee grinder.

Believe a pound of butter adds gloss
to the frosting.

Be grateful. Once there were epochs
with no ingredients for cake.

The dog that won't cross over

That's what they call him, he confides. *Every time we go to the vet. The diagnosis was cancer almost two years ago. He was only supposed to last six months. Mind you, we can't go anywhere. He keeps us home. It's a sort-of palliative care, you might say. We have him on a high protein diet, and sometimes we hand-feed him. He's been such a great little dog; we couldn't give up on him. You know what it's like. He's got his meds and he sleeps a lot. We won't get another one for a while.*

spring rain
the orange ball
in last year's leaves

My sister in the cemetery

she crouches, as if reverent,
knees bent; her eyes cast upward
she is light-lured, how sun gilds the edge
of stone shoulders, the wedge of heel to toe,
shadow, in deep folds, fingers,
how moss adheres and velvets spaces,
all the resting places, immortalizing surnames
her camera frames the mourning statuary
solitary

Small hands

They say there are three deaths:
when your body stops, when you're lowered
into the grave, and the last time your name is spoken.

You have no names. As others boast
of grandchildren, we say, someday. You are bequeathed:
toys boxed in the attic, scuffed baby shoes, knit blankets.

Let there be three births: the thought, the act, the you.

The year I was born they buried a Plymouth Belvedere

It happened in Oklahoma, in a large hole in the courthouse lawn.
With it went 10 gallons of gasoline, a case of beer
and the contents of a woman's handbag in the glove compartment:
lipstick, pack of gum, tissues, cigarettes, matches, $2.43
and a bottle of tranquilizers.
Fifty years later, lifting the car from the concrete vault,
after pumping out half a metre of water,
they wonder if it will start, calling it a fairy tale,
"our King Tut's tomb", this gold and white two-door hardtop
a celebration of Oklahoma's statehood.
I contemplate my own fiftieth. A beaded hospital bracelet,
baptismal certificate, a pill bottle of baby teeth:
artifacts of me that my mother kept in a drawer.
Someone fifty years ago guessed Tulsa's population for 2007
to win the secret Belvedere, like some child's pirate-dream.
A buried baseball card, a silver dollar, a girlfriend's name,
a cigar box crypt in an empty field.
A birthday of revelation and concealment, of forgetting and forging ahead,
unwilling to be some future's novelty of age.

Acknowledgements

Some of these poems, or earlier versions, have appeared in the following: *The New Quarterly*, and Leaf Press chapbooks from Patrick Lane's poetry retreats at Glenairley, Ocean Wilderness and Honeymoon Bay. Thanks to Ursula Vaira, the gathered poets, and Patrick.

"M PATHY" won an honourable mention in the Genjuan International Haibun Contest in Japan, 2017, and was published in the anthology, *Cottage of Visions, Decorated works 2015-2017*.

The book's title is a reference to Edna St. Vincent Millay's poem, "Sorrow". (*Sorrow like a ceaseless rain beats upon my heart…*)

I first read about the ortolan bunting in Nicole Bestard's poem, "Ortolan", *Rattle #28*.

The idea for Lapis lazuli came from an article, "Medieval women's early involvement in manuscript production suggested by lapis lazuli identification in dental calculus", *Science Advances*, 09 Jan. 2019.

The format of the sevenling for small hands was inspired by Anna Akhmatova's poem translated by D.M. Thomas, as used by Roddy Lumsden. The idea of three deaths is attributed to David Eagleman.

The phrase, "map of sorrow", is used by C.S. Lewis in *A Grief Observed*.

My admiration to Hospice staff and volunteers.

Thank you to Dawn for her keen eye and sensibility; preventing haibun from becoming halibut. Thank you Aimee.

Author Biography

Dorothy Mahoney is the author of three poetry collections, *Through Painted Skies* (Black Moss Press, 1997), *Returning to the Point* (Black Moss Press, 2001), and *Off-Leash* (Palimpsest Press, 2016). Her poetry has been included in numerous journals and anthologies, including *Detours: An Anthology of Poets from Windsor and Essex County, Erotic Haiku,* and *Because We Have All Lived Here.* A retired teacher, she resides in Windsor, Ontario.

PHOTO CREDIT: GREG MAHONEY